Trading Mind-Sets

God, Faith, and Disability

Trading Mind-Sets

God, Faith, and Disability

Joe Boyd

TTA International

TTA International Ltd
Hatfield Avenue, Fleetwood, England.

ISBN 978-1-9993316-2-7

CONTENTS

ACKNOWLEDGEMENTS

I am as proud of this work as I have been of anything I have written over the past twenty-five years. Putting it together has challenged me occupationally, spiritually, and physically.

Once again, I would like to thank Alistair Bates and the team at Timeless Publications for giving me the opportunity to pen 'the book I have always wanted to write.' I am eternally grateful to my best friend of fifteen years, Maggie Jordan, who patiently proofread the original transcript for me. Thanks are also due to Erin Brown, whose editing work continues to make the musings of this ageing journalist palatable to a wider audience.

I send my love to the children of Castle Tower Special School in Ballymena, whom I pray will benefit from the proceeds of *Trading Mind-Sets*.

My heart is abounding with love for my beautiful wife, Rachael, my mother and father, Stanley and Margaret Boyd, and my grandmother, Agnes Maxwell, who have spent their lives caring selflessly for me and others. Remembered with affection too are my late grandfather, Willie

Maxwell, and my mother-in-law, Olive. Not forgetting my father-in-law, Sydney.

Crucially, I praise my Lord and Saviour, Jesus Christ, who made me, sustains me, and blesses me with amazing people and opportunities. I love you, Lord. To You be the glory.

INTRODUCTION

'Right Here, Right Now' 'Real Real Real'

Ironic or what? A Christian author starts his book with a chapter title using two song titles by early '90s indie band Jesus Jones. Blasphemous? Maybe it's my ego, my wanting to be an 'International Bright Young Thing' in publishing circles? Okay, enough with the puns.

Believe it or not, I am going somewhere with this. I sit in front of my laptop as a forty-two-year-old journalist, still basking in the glory of my recently published autobiography, *Trading Places: From Hopelessness to Happiness*. I am eager to keep the writing-career momentum going. I have spent my morning composing and sending publicity releases to every magazine I can think of in an effort to keep selling the thing. Having written and emailed articles, my mind won't rest. Something that my fellow Timeless scribbler Alistair Bates said to me as he delivered the first consignment of *Trading Places*.

"Ready for book two?" he asked, flashing a smile.

"Steady on," I said.

In truth, I had been mulling over ideas for a follow-up. Alistair's question added fuel to my thoughts, and now my mind won't stop running with several possibilities.

Tuesday, 21 April 2019, I am still officially off work for the Easter holidays. I could listen to Spotify, watch some DVDs, eat chocolate, or go for a walk. But no, I must test this idea for a new book. Is it from God, or is it about my wanting to be more than a 'one book wonder'? Am I on a selfish quest to see my name in print for a second time, or does God have something else to say, using me as the vessel? Time will tell . . . or rather, He will.

Believe it or not, the outlandish Introduction title succinctly conveys my thoughts. Physically, I am feeling pretty awful! My spine is causing me so much pain that I cannot sit up straight in my swivel chair. I need to perch with a slight bend in my back. 'Flexion for comfort' the school physios used to call it. My knee joints are sore with a burning pain that stretches down to my ankle joints. The same is true of the hinge joint that carries the bridge from my elbows to my wrists. I wish I could lay down.

In theory, there is nothing to stop me from doing so. No employer I have ever written for has forced me to work. Indeed, my former editor at the *Ballymena Times* newspaper, Dessie Blackadder, once threatened to send me home after I had arrived back from a short walk too exhausted to move.

My wife, Rachael, has just texted from work to inquire about my day. Learning of my pain, she asks if I have taken my medication. I fib that I have, telling only a partial lie. The truth is, I would love to take something to relieve these aches, but I can't face the journey from my study to the adjacent room where my pills are!

However, as always, a voice or a drive, call it what you will, urges me to continue writing, to keep going. For now, I will feel no peace in my spirit until I do.

I have four reasons for writing *Trading Mind-Sets: God, Faith, and Disability*.

Firstly, I want to unpack what the Bible has to say about the causes of disability and illness. Is disability part of God's plan for the world He created and the people therein? If not, what happened to cause its occurrence? All, I hope, will be revealed.

Secondly, I want to look at some of the competing mind-sets on disability that were on display in Bible times. Initially, I will look at how people in ancient times saw others with disabilities. Then I will outline how Jesus regarded those who live with physical or learning disabilities, for want of a better word.

Thirdly, I will look at what the Bible has to say about disability and healing. Again, I believe that God's Word is very clear on this topic.

Finally, I will again use God's Word and the experiences He has allowed in my life to respectfully offer encouragement to individuals who are living with a restricting condition. Can the Lord really use such people in His kingdom, even to the point of turning their situations round for good? I believe so and will explain why.

I pray when you read this book, whether you are a pastor, caregiver, disability professional, or person who has a condition, you will gain insight on this important topic. Perhaps this book will be your catalyst to 'trade in' your current views on disability and the Word in exchange for a fresh mind-set.

However, before we learn what the Bible says about this massive subject of disability, it is important to define the term as it is generally understood by most people. For this reason, the secular mind-set on disability will form the first chapter of this book.

In presenting my thoughts, I am conscious that we all experience disability in a variety of ways. A professional whom I respect once wrote, 'Cerebral palsy affects 1 in 1000 people and no two children are affected in quite the same way.'[1] Over the years, I have come to realise the accuracy of her statement.

Although you may not agree with everything I say in this book, I certainly do not want to offend anyone. However, having lived with cerebral palsy all of my life, I do offer keen insight into disability. I state the truth as I understand it, for to do otherwise runs contrary to my faith and the Saviour who inspires it.

Okay. I give in! Before I write anymore, my brain and body are finally in agreement. I need my meds and a nap! Keep reading while I shut my eyes for a few moments.

CHAPTER ONE

'WHAT'S WRONG WITH YOU?'

The Secular Mind-Set on Disability

If I could charge a penny every time I have been asked 'What's wrong with you?' I would never have to work again. While that question is in itself rude, what's worse are crude labels to denote disabilities: 'spaz', 'crip', 'unfortunate', or, to use the current socially acceptable label, 'person with a disability'. I've heard them all ad nauseam.

What does the world say is 'wrong' with Joe Boyd? According to the United Kingdom Equality Act of 2010, I have a disability because my body is impacted by a condition which is accepted as 'physical or mental impairment that has a "substantial" and "long-term" negative effect on your ability to do normal daily activities.'[1]

In my case, I was born with what is referred to in medical textbooks as 'spastic diplegia'. My disability occurred when my brain was starved of oxygen for about a minute during my birth. My prematurely hatched self was unable to cope with life outside the womb without medical support for a time.

In layman's term, I have a form of cerebral palsy. Put simply, it is a kind of paralysis in my cerebellum. This causes the messages from my brain to the parts of my body that control limb movement to become muddled. It is made worse when I am tired so that even my speech is affected. Consequently, I walk with a pronounced stagger. On a good day, I can walk unaided for short distances, but I often use a rollator to help me keep my balance. I occasionally use a wheelchair for comfort and safety on big excursions.

If I am really exhausted, my neck muscles twitch, causing my head to move in whatever way it pleases, be this up and down, round and round, or side to side. At that point, my speech becomes slow and slurred, my motor skills are sluggish, and a lie-down is necessary.

I am blessed with a high level of academic and social intelligence, although the part of my brain that adjudicates on distance is wonky, making driving impossible and crossing roads a fraught experience. Disorientation in crowds affects me, so when I indulge my passion for live music, I prefer to be accompanied by my wife, Rachael, my mum, or a friend.

Limited hand movement causes my handwriting to resemble that of a child, and a lack of fine motor control in my fingers makes tying my shoelaces or knotting a tie an unfathomable task.

My pain levels vary from day to day. Sometimes I move around with relative ease. Other times, even sitting up in a chair is too painful—my knees and spine can't hold me up, and I must rest.

This is, of course, my personal experience of disability and how it affects me. Each person who has a restrictive condition will report at least some variation in experiences, however slight.

I am not a physician, and *Trading Mind-Sets* is not a medical book. Therefore, I do not have the knowledge or ambition to outline every form of disability or its causes. There are numerous forms of physical disability: spina bifida and hydrocephalus (a hole in the spine and fluid on the brain, respectively), muscular dystrophy (progressive weakness in the muscles), multiple sclerosis (and other conditions which affect the body and nervous system), just to name a few.

On a different note, phrases such as 'mental handicap' and 'retard' have been replaced by an all-compassing term called 'learning disability'. I believe that dropping words like 'retard' or 'mental' is a very good idea on account of the negative connotations they contain. However, I do not think that their standardised replacement is very useful either. I would even argue that to label a large group of people as having a 'learning disability' creates more issues than it solves. I reckon it is because the term fails to make an adequate distinction between individuals who are slightly less able to learn but able-bodied in every other way and others who have a more noticeable issue such as Down syndrome.

In recent years, attempts have been made to create a distinction by using the words *mild to moderate learning disability* to refer to people who may previously have been labelled 'slow to learn', as I once was. *Severe learning disability* covers men and women affected by Downs and other severe issues. Whilst any attempt at effective distinction is to be welcomed, I still have concerns that Joe Public will fail to grasp these subtle terminology changes and continue to generalise. I fear this uneducated perception of the nature of disability will lead to fewer or limited opportunities for those on the more able side of the learning difficulties spectrum.

So far, I have spoken about my own disability and others in the context of what has been traditionally referred to as 'the medical model'. In a nutshell, this view of disability establishes the person as being afflicted with some impairment or restriction which requires intervention, correction, or care.

Since the late 1970s, as people with disabilities have become more empowered and educated, we've seen a move towards 'a social model' of disability. Academics such as Mike Oliver who are disabled have argued that it is society which creates and perpetuates disability by creating and maintaining barriers and attitudes that restrict opportunities for people with disabilities. According to this viewpoint, the impact of disability can be removed if the physical barriers or prejudicial attitudes that make life opportunities inaccessible to people with disabilities are removed or challenged.

Even more recent disability theorists have suggested, as I understand it, an end to the distinction between 'able-bodied' and 'disabled' people. Their argument states that everyone faces an issue which limits them to some degree; therefore, each person is 'disabled' in some way.

I do understand where the supporters of each model of disability are coming from. For example, many able-bodied people experience problems and issues in life which cause as much heartache, pain, and frustration as my cerebral palsy (CP) creates for me. Personal life experience has also shown me that my physical difficulties are lessened when I am able to go to the cinema, enjoy a meal out, or attend a concert in which the building is devoid of stairs and the staff is helpful. The 'medical model' has its critics, but, in my educated opinion, it is impossible to deny that I, and others with a physical disability, experience bodily pain which those without a disability do not. Disability in any form can be congenital (that is, born with an impairment) or acquired (disabled as a result of an illness or accident).

I have gone around the houses, but to answer 'What is wrong with you?', my body is affected by the physical symptoms of cerebral palsy. My ability to function may be helped or hindered by the physical accessibility of my surroundings and the attitudes of the people therein. My physical limitations are painful and frustrating, but I am conscious and empathic towards others who also struggle.

The medical, social, or other models of disability are useful as a starting point to the discussion regarding the subject because they offer a basic understanding of what disability is and how it is talked about, something that is particularly useful for people who may know little about the topic. However, these present models provide only a partial, even negative, view on the topic of disability. The most important and effective model in living effectively with a disability is found in the Bible, God's Word.

Choosing to turn to the next page may educate, enlighten, encourage, or infuriate you, but for anyone who has ever asked me, 'What's wrong with you?', all will certainly be revealed.

CHAPTER TWO

A NASTY FALL

The Biblical View on the Cause of Disability

Anyone who knew me as a teenager would tell you that I was as stubborn as a colony of mules. I refused to wear splints or to use a wheelchair . . . or any kind of walking aid to maintain my balance. I reasoned that using this equipment would mark me as being even more different from my able-bodied peers than I already appeared to be. I wasn't having any of that.

Looking back, my thinking was daft. Not being the most stable walker, I frequently landed on my backside. While I purposed to maintain the appearance that I was just as big and strong as everyone else, the effort became too much.

Remarkably, forty-two years of falls have resulted in only two broken toes and a few bumps, bruises, and several episodes of hurt pride.

Why I was born with cerebral palsy and others have received various forms of disability is due directly to humanity's biggest tumble ever recorded . . . long before I was ever conceived.

Genesis 3 outlines the events described in God's Word as 'the fall'. This is when the first human beings, Adam (a name possibly derived from the Hebrew word *Adamah*, meaning 'earth') and Eve, 'mother of all the living' (v. 20), disobeyed God's direct instruction not to eat from the Tree of the Knowledge of Good and Evil. God's enemy, Satan, appeared in the form of a serpent and tempted Eve: 'Did God really say, "You must not eat from any tree in the garden?"' (v. 1).

In the following line, Eve issues the correct reply: 'We may eat fruit from the trees in the garden, but God did say, "You must not eat fruit from the tree that is in the middle of the garden, and you must not touch it, or you will die"' (vv. 2–3).

Ever cunning, the devil then proceeds to twist God's words by lying to Eve about the consequences of consuming the forbidden fruit. '"You will not die," he said. "Eating from that tree will make you like God, wise, knowing the difference between right and wrong"' (vv. 4–5, author's paraphrase). Satan intimated that having such knowledge is to be desired.

Appealing to Eve's ego worked. Verse 6 tells us that Eve's eyes were drawn to the fruit. Her curiosity and desire for knowledge kindled, she consumed the fruit from the Tree of the Knowledge of Good and Evil. Then she gave some to Adam, who also had a bite. At the very moment, the game was up. Death and decay, pain and suffering entered the world. For some, one consequence would manifest itself as disability.

Prior to that first sin, the fall, the world and everything in it were flawless. For proof of this, look with me at the story of creation in Genesis. In Genesis 1, we read that over a period of six days, God spoke the world into existence, beginning with light which He separated into day and night (v. 1) and continued with the sky; land; sun, moon, and stars; living creatures, including birds, animals, and insects (vv. 6–25). Each time God completed every act of creation, He saw it and pronounced what He had made to be 'good' (vv. 3, 9, 11, 18, 21, 25, and 31). He didn't say it was 'all right' or 'needed improvement', but 'good'. His final act of creation was human beings. We enjoy the unique privilege of being made in the image of God (v. 27). He appointed humans to 'rule' over the earth and every creature on it.

In Genesis 2, we also discover that 'four headwaters' flowed from the river which watered the garden. One of these flowed to the land of Havilah, in which there was gold, aromatic resin, and onyx (vv. 10–12.) As I write this on May 2019, when many of the world's economies are facing bankruptcy, to be living in a luscious garden in which gold and expensive commodities existed in abundance paints a picture of how perfectly God created the world.

God placed Adam in the garden to take care of it (v. 15). Work was intended to be a pleasurable act of service to the Creator. Marriage was a loving partnership meant to relieve loneliness and meet the human need for love and companionship.

Consider all of this in light of what is said elsewhere in Scripture about God's perfection: '[God] is the Rock, his works are perfect, and all his ways are just. A faithful God who does no wrong, upright and just is he' (Deut. 32:4).

It is no exaggeration to describe the world as paradise prior to Adam and Eve's terrible failure. Pain, soreness, and limitation did not exist in the beginning. Wheelchairs, crutches, and pain-relieving medication were not needed to get around in the garden of Eden.

This perfect situation changed only as a result of human sinfulness. Returning to Genesis 3, we discover other consequences of the fall besides sin. Pain would become part and parcel of pregnancy and childbirth (v. 16). Work, whilst bringing rewards, would also become painful toil which would tire, age, and weaken our bodies that will ultimately return to dust (vv. 17–19). Access to the Tree of Life was blocked by a flaming sword (v. 24). And so began humanity's problems, one of which is suffering and limitation.

'Now, wait a minute, Joe,' you say. 'I have a disability [or an illness], but I never disobeyed a direct instruction from God. I have asked for knowledge on a par with His, yet I am stuck with my limitations. God is a nasty bully who is punishing me for something that isn't my fault.'

Have you ever cursed? Have you ever had a malicious thought? Have you resented someone or lost your temper, even for a nanosecond? Perhaps you have wanted something that wasn't yours? Answer yes to any of these questions and you, too, are guilty of sin, just as Adam and Eve were. Wrongdoing is wrongdoing, full stop, and the Bible is unambiguous when it comes to disobedience: 'For whoever keeps the whole law and yet stumbles at just one point is guilty of breaking all of it' (James 2:10).

You are, therefore, just as deserving as anyone else of experiencing pain, illness, disability, or any other symptom of a broken world. You are no more deserving but, certainly, no less.

When presenting my position in the past, members of the disabled community who are proud of their life circumstances have jumped on my statement and berated me for daring to suggest that disability comes from the devil. First, if this describes you, I commend you for having such an unrelentingly positive attitude towards your condition. My admiration and envy in equal measure are yours! But before I respond to the suggestion that the devil caused the disability or illness, I would ask another question: Has your condition ever caused you a moment's pain, discomfort, or frustration? If so, then you have been impacted, however briefly, by Satan, otherwise known as the devil. He is described as 'the father of lies' (John 8:44). The whole world is 'under the power of the wicked one' (1 John 5:19).

If we accept the viewpoint that disability occurs in our bodies as a result of a fallen world, the prognosis for those affected may, at first glance, appear bleak. According to this, it is arguably true that people with disabilities should be viewed as victims of a sad situation, causalities of spiritual warfare. For decades, disability campaigners have argued that those with a physical or learning-related condition were viewed in ways that did little to maximise their opportunities or talents. Many, if not all, of these competing/overlapping perspectives were on display in biblical times.

The differing attitudes and ideas on disability fall into five broad and sometimes overlapping categories.

1. People with disabilities are a homogeneous yet alien group destined to exist outside of mainstream society.
2. People with disabilities are treated as objects of shame or viewed as useless by society and, thus, are prone to a form of self-

loathing which manifests itself through low self-esteem.

3. People with disabilities are vulnerable, objects of pity, needing more care and compassion than others and essentially have little or no ability to participate in the real world.
4. People with disabilities are more inspiring than others, worthy of extra praise and are somehow 'special'.
5. People with disabilities are made in the image of God, deserving of care and love as human beings, with a responsibility to live life to the best of their ability.

These 'mind-sets' on disability are evident today just as they were in the Bible. This is surely proof, if any were needed, that the writer of Ecclesiastes was spot-on when he said: 'What has been will be again, what has been done will be done again; there is nothing new under the sun' (1:9).

CHAPTER THREE

'ARE THEY FRIENDS OF YOURS?'

A Homogenous Mind-Set on Disability

Several years ago, I called into the fast-food restaurant for lunch on my way to college. As the waitress served my food, she asked, 'Are you going to sit over there with the rest of them?' She glanced towards a table where young people wearing the uniform of a school for children with severe learning disabilities were seated.

I smiled. 'No. I'd like my food to-go.'

My heart sank. How could someone who had never met me assume that I was part of a learning-disabled group just because I walked with a limp? My frustration quickly gave way to acceptance. It wasn't the first time that I, a university graduate and working journalist, had been impacted by a similar assumption.

It got me thinking about a colony of lepers Jesus met as he travelled from Samaria to Galilee. The story is found in Luke 17:11–19. This group of people had contracted a highly painful and contagious skin disease. Arguably worse than the physical agony they endured was their exclusion from society because of the illness that afflicted them. Separation of people with a contagious disease from society had been sanctioned for the protection of the local population, suppressing the afflicted individuals' unique characteristics and superseding their need for love, affection, and care. Only a complete cure from their leprosy, which the local priest could verify, would be enough to allow them back into mainstream society. Their cry for mercy was heartfelt and would ultimately be life changing, for Jesus healed them (v. 14).

A 'legion' of demons possessed the man in Mark 5:7, imprisoning him in constant torment and forcing him to live in caves. Naked, demented, alone, and bleeding from numerous self-inflicted cuts (v. 5), he, too, remained outside of society because of a severe physical and mental condition.

A further glance into God's Word reveals that disability or illness and its impact were not restricted to people on the margins of society. In 2 Kings 5, we read about Naaman, who was 'commander of the army of the king of Aram'. He was 'a great man in the sight of his master' and accustomed to victory in battle. Yet he had leprosy and sought healing from God through the Lord's anointed prophet Elisha (vv. 2–9).

Even the greatest of biblical kings were not immune from disability and marginalisation. Nebuchadnezzar was the longest-serving and, arguably, most powerful emperor in Babylonian history. Yet when he was overcome by mental illness, we read that he was 'driven away from people and ate grass like an ox' (Dan. 4:33). Nebuchadnezzar's problems occurred as a result of his own arrogance and failure to acknowledge that it was the Lord who had blessed him so richly, whereas Naaman's disease was not due to anything he had or had not done.

My point is that in Bible times, as now, people with disabilities are sometimes viewed purely in terms of their conditions. Their humanity and individual needs were and are sometimes overlooked. They are viewed and treated as one big homogeneous group. Even more dangerous is that they are deemed as 'other', in the sense of being outside of what is considered 'normal' even when they are able to fully function within society.

I suggest that adopting what I term as a *homogeneous perspective* on disability does not align with God's view. In Psalm 139:14, David exalts God: 'I praise you because I am fearfully and wonderfully made; your works are wonderful, I know that full well.' David's inspired words indicate that people with disabilities are as 'fearfully and wonderfully made' as other human beings—no more and no less. The implication is that God makes each individual and gives them a unique role to play in His plan. As image bearers of their Creator, their uniqueness is to be recognised.

Being wonderfully made excludes disabled people from being pitied for their conditions. Equally true, even profound, is a second mind-set: individuals falling into self-pity because of their afflictions create additional problems while wasting precious moments that could be better spent fulfilling their God-given purpose.

The key problem that self-pity causes for people will disabilities with regard to the person themselves is that he or she comes to believe that they are 'useless' and 'incapable', with the result that they lose the motivation to actively live the life they have been given, believing that all they can do it sit in a corner and be babysat, looking to others to meet their functional needs.

Falling into the 'self-pity' trap can also be problematic for the companions of those with disabilities as they may become downhearted by the inability of their loved one to see a reason to function or try to live that demonstrates their 'wonderfully made' selves.

Self-pity or pity that others may offer you on account of your condition is condescending and unhelpful, as you will discover in the next chapter. Meanwhile, the antidote is to avoid seeing yourself as part of the homogeneous group of helpless people and recognising your individuality and uniqueness in Christ.

CHAPTER FOUR

'AT LEAST HE'S LOYAL'

A Pitiful Mind-Set on Disability

My teenage years were spent being a proud member of the Junior branch of the local Orange Order. As such, I had the opportunity to participate in many of the parades in which my lodge took part in throughout the summer marching season.

During one early summer parade in Ballymena, my mum and I were sitting with the crowd waiting for my fellow Orange men at the start of the march. Dressed in my Orange Order collarette, I sat in my wheelchair. A couple of elderly ladies came over to us and looked down at me with sad eyes. One said to her companion and my mum, 'Ah, God love him. At least he is loyal.' With this, the lady and her friend turned and walked away.

The woman's pitiful facial expression and pronouncement conveyed her thinking about people with disabilities. She seemed to feel sorry for me in my physical state, believing that I was just a poor wee boy in a wheelchair whose most positive attribute was being a loyal Protestant.

Of course, showing mercy and compassion for someone who is having trouble is not wrong. Indeed, certain translations of the Bible, for example, the Contemporary English Version, say that blind Bartimaeus cried out to Jesus, saying, 'Jesus, Son of David, have pity on me!' (Mark 10:47). The story goes on to describe the interaction between Jesus and Bartimaeus. Jesus asked him what he would like Him to do. Bartimaeus requested the ability to see again, a heartfelt plea which our merciful Saviour God granted. I believe that anyone with a physical disability in the same situation, myself included, would have asked for relief from their affliction, rightly so.

However, there is a difference between having genuine compassion for someone, which leads to positive action on their behalf, and pity, which is nothing more than an indulgent feeling sorry for and patronising one who is experiencing problems but without looking to help their situation in any meaningful way.

A quick look at the book of Job explains why coming alongside someone in physical, mental, or emotional distress with a pity-filled mind-set is unhelpful. In fact, this kind of thinking makes the person who is offering 'pity' part of the problem.

In the opening chapters, we meet Job, a wealthy and healthy man who followed and obeyed God with enviable diligence. God Himself goes as far as to say, 'There is no one on earth like him; he is blameless and upright, a man who fears God and shuns evil' (1:8). Such was the Lord's confidence in Job's righteousness that He invites Satan to test his faithfulness. Firstly, the devil removed Job's wealth: herds of oxen, donkeys, sheep, and camels (vv. 13–17). Then Satan caused the death of his sons and daughters (vv. 18–19). Subsequently, Satan was permitted to affect Job's body so that he broke out in sores from the top of his head to the soles of his feet (2:7).

Later chapters inform us that three of Job's friends rushed to his side, no doubt with the intention of offering comfort and instruction which, they thought, would enable their stricken companion to get his life back on track. Eliphaz the Temanite was the first to step forward. 'You have instructed many . . . now trouble comes to you, and you are discouraged . . . [were not] your blameless ways your hope?' (4:3–6). If you were Job, would these words have encouraged you? Likely not! Perhaps most upsetting to Job was Eliphaz's additional advice in verse 7: 'Those who plough evil and those who sow trouble reap it.'

A second friend, Bildad the Shuhite, was equally unhelpful to Job. 'Does the Almighty pervert what is right?' (8:30), he asks, then adds that if Job 'seeks God earnestly' and is 'pure and upright', he will be restored to prosperity (v. 5–6).

Zophar the Naamathite is perhaps the least helpful of all Job's supposed comforters. He suggests to his suffering friend that 'life will be brighter than the noonday' (11:17) if Job will 'put away the sin that is in your hand' (v. 14).

Job's friends arrived with sympathy and sought to offer sincere advice and comfort. However, their well-intentioned interventions caused more harm than good as they lacked a basic understanding of God's character. It is impossible for the Lord, being entirely good in character, to cause Job's financial issues, personal grief, or physical illness. That is the province of the devil.

His companions' lack of knowledge led to ill-judged advice, which made Job feel even worse about his situation, just as the lady with pity-filled eyes and thoughtless words caused me to feel much smaller than the teenager I was. My own experience of being on the receiving end of this well-meaning but flawed attention that makes one feel 'not enough' can lead to self-esteem issues and feelings of unworthiness. Offering platitudes to a person with a disability can tempt him or her to fall into the even more dangerous trap of self-pity.

This mind-set towards fellow image bearers is not as Christ desires, for he came that we might have life and 'have it to the full' (John 10:10). He never added conditions to His promise. It is for all His people.

While the book of Job is careful to record that the protagonist did not 'sin by charging God with wrongdoing' (1:22), he was guilty of succumbing to self-pity regarding his circumstances. 'Why did I not perish at birth, and die as I came into the womb?' he moans (3:11). He talks of feeling 'wronged' by God, and says, 'Though I cry, "Violence!" I get no response; though I call for help, there is no justice. He has blocked my way so I cannot pass; he has shrouded my paths in darkness' (vv. 7 –8).

Towards the end of the chapter, we find God challenging Job by reminding him who holds the ultimate authority: 'Where were you when I laid the earth's foundation? Tell me, if you understand' (38:4). 'Do you know when the mountain goats give birth? Do you watch when the doe bears her fawn?' (39:1).

By chapter 40, Job is forced to concede. 'I am unworthy—how can I reply to you? I put my hand over my mouth. I spoke once, but I have no answer—twice, but I will say no more' (vv. 4–5).

At this, Satan backs down from his challenge. Job is, as God said, 'blameless and upright, a man who fears God and shuns evil' (1:8). The God of compassion rained down more blessings than ever on Job's life, rendering his self-pity moot. 'The Lord blessed the latter part of Job's life more than the former part. He had fourteen thousand sheep, six thousand camels, a thousand yoke of oxen and a thousand donkeys. And he also had seven sons and three daughters. . . . and their father granted them an inheritance along with their brother' (vv. 12–15). Job's restoration to better circumstances, including additional children, showed a God who delights in blessing His people through and after difficult times.

Unfortunately, notions that physical or learning impairments are shameful continue to create a heart-breaking impact on not only the people with disabilities and their families and friends but also the world as well.

CHAPTER FIVE

'HE DIDN'T GET IT FROM OUR SIDE OF THE HOUSE'

A Shame-Filled Mind-Set on Disability

When I was diagnosed with cerebral palsy in the late 1970s, one elderly relative responded, 'He didn't get that from our side of the house.' I am reluctant to be critical of this person since she showed me great love throughout her life. Granted, this statement was typical of the time. However, it illustrates the idea that having a disability is not only at odds with what is considered 'normal' but also a scenario from which people wish to distance themselves, even when they are close to the person affected. I call this thought pattern a shame-filled mind-set on disability.

When disability is viewed through eyes of shame, the person with the condition is often excluded from activities and situations that able-bodied people access without a second thought. For example, I was once strongly advised not to go on a weekend excursion with friends from church as my usual carer feared that I would be a 'burden' to other people on the trip. Her words planted the seed in my mind that I was somehow not worthy to participate in the trip because I had a physical disability and would need help to get around. In hindsight, I now see that the carer was trying to shield me from possible rejection by friends who might have concluded that having to support me was too much of a chore. However, what I understood then was that having cerebral palsy made me a 'problem'. I felt ashamed of my circumstances.

In Mark 10:46–52, we find someone with a physical limitation who was treated as an object of unworthiness because of his disability. Bartimaeus, whom we mentioned in the previous chapter, was blind. 'Jesus, Son of David, have mercy on me' (v. 47), he cried as the Saviour and His disciples arrived in Jericho. The crowd had something to say to his outburst. 'Many rebuked him and told him to be quiet' (v. 48).

It is my assumption that those who scolded Bartimaeus thought of him as a nuisance and were of the opinion that someone as important as Jesus would not have the time or desire to pander to the shouts of a blind man. Thankfully, verse 48 goes on to say that Bartimaeus 'shouted all more.' Perhaps this is why there is a happy ending to the story when his request 'to see' (v. 51) is met with the news that his faith in Jesus as a healer had made him well. I have read this passage countless times over my forty-two years and have never failed to shout: 'Go, Jesus!' or 'Get in, Bartimaeus.' I am, truth be told, a little envious, particularly during my most painful moments, that Bartimaeus received full healing here on earth.

The same spirit of covetousness sometimes comes upon me when I read about how Jesus moved to heal the ten lepers (Luke 17:11–19) or the two demon-possessed men (Matt. 8:28–34). In both scenarios, mainstream society had excluded them based on their physical/mental illnesses, deeming them unable to participate in 'normal' life. Their conditions forced them into isolation and, I am sure, loneliness. The lepers who were healed received relief from the physical effects of their illness while the demon-possessed men returned to a sound state of mind. More than this, however, is that each one was granted a passport back into 'normal' life. They could once again live in a home in the close company of family and friends and be accepted as equals. They no longer had to deal with the shame of having a condition that forced them to be separated from society or feel like second-class citizens.

The same was true of Bartimaeus. His healing brought not only sight but also the potential that people would treat him as an equal, not simply someone who needed to 'be quiet' while an important person passed by.

My life experiences, reading the Bible, and researching the social aspect of living with a disability have revealed that not only are those with disabilities sometimes viewed with embarrassment and shame but also their circumstances may affect how they think of themselves. I call this the self-loathing perspective, which, as we are about to see, is as negative as it sounds.

CHAPTER SIX

'I'M NOT WORTHY'

A Self-Loathing Mind-Set on Disability

In preparation for writing this book, I surveyed over one hundred people with disabilities. My goal was to gain the most accurate picture of the problems facing people with impairments. Even a cursory glance at the responses indicates that the biggest problem I and my fellow members of the disabled community face is a lack of belief or confidence in ourselves and our abilities.

One woman I talked to is in her mid-twenties. Her noticeable physical disability has not stopped her from living on her own, driving, and graduating twice, with a third qualification on the way. Yet she reports that her experiences within both a special school and a mainstream one, which she felt was ill-equipped to meet her needs, have left her with what she describes as 'anxiety issues which affect me to this day.'

I can relate. Although I have graduated, married, and worked as a reporter for nearly twenty-five years, I will admit that an eminent paediatrician's conclusion about me when I was fourteen haunts me even today. She wrote, 'Joseph's intelligence is below normal' before going on to suggest that I was 'slow to learn.'

Early on, her assessment spurred me to excel during my student and early working years. However, as time progressed, her lingering pronouncement has continued to drive my thinking that I must be working, writing, and publishing regularly to *prove my worth*. I do not like to fail to reach any of the goals I set for myself, no matter how extreme and difficult they may be. I understand that this is not the attitude with which God wants me to approach life. But it is a fact that people with disabilities are often beset by low self-esteem as a result of life experiences emanating from their conditions.

Moses, whom God chose to lead the Israelites out of slavery in Egypt, is a clear biblical example of someone who nearly allowed his disability, a speech impediment, to obstruct the Lord's plans for him. In Exodus 4:10, we find the man who would perhaps become Israel's greatest leader asking God to send someone else to confront Pharaoh because he was 'slow of speech and tongue.' Moses's self-esteem may have been so eroded by his speech impairment and the shame he may have experienced because of it that he felt ill-equipped to lead the nation of Israel

A lack of self-esteem on account of having a disability is evident in a woman who had been suffering from severe bleeding for twelve years (Mark 8:25–34). Verse 26 notes that she had spent all of her money consulting numerous doctors (an expensive process in those times) but never finding relief. By the time she met Jesus, all of her wealth had evaporated, yet she still suffered from the malady. Her shame is evidenced by the fact that she didn't face Jesus and ask for healing. Instead, she seemed to feel able only to touch the hem of His cloak in hopes of receiving healing. What's more, when Jesus sensed power going out from Him, He turned to the woman. She spoke to Jesus, 'trembling with fear', in the wake of her healing, possibly expecting Him to be angry at her for accessing His power without permission. Of course, His response, 'Daughter, your faith has healed you. Go in peace and be freed from your suffering' assure her that the Lord was anything but cross.

What a blessing for someone who had suffered for so long. However, approaching Jesus as she reluctantly did indicates that her illness had made her fearful of stepping out to get help. After all, no one had helped her in all those years. Anyone who has lost hope and is considered by society as 'unclean', as she was, understandably takes a hit to their self-esteem. I can only imagine that she saw Jesus as her final chance for a physical cure.

I commend the high level of faith in Jesus she obviously possessed. This led her to a realisation that even the slightest touch from Jesus could transform her life. She was right!

Of course, it is not only pity from others or a lack of self-esteem that creates problems for people with disabilities. Others' mind-sets that see us as vulnerable, objects of shame, useless, or even 'inspirational' can stop disabled people from realising their full, God-given potential. In my experience, seeing those with disabilities as vulnerable is the most common mind-set.

CHAPTER SEVEN

'I JUST DON'T WANT YOU GETTING HURT'

A Vulnerable Mind-set on Disability

The 'vulnerable mind-set on disability' refers to the belief that disabled people are more likely to experience rejection, exploitation, or injury because their condition causes them to be physically/emotionally more fragile than someone who is able-bodied. You might wonder how is one's physical/emotional nature made more vulnerable by the impact their conditions both now and in the biblical area.

Again, this topic resonates with me. Often when I was a little boy, the adults who looked after me were reluctant to let me participate in some of the activities with other children who did not have a disability.

'What if you can't do it, Joseph?' they said. Or, 'What if you end up getting hurt?'

I grew quite tired of hearing these two questions. All I wanted to do was be like the 'normal' youngsters, but I wasn't allowed because I was perceived as vulnerable to injury. There may have been a degree of truth in what the grown-ups were saying, but I couldn't see it at the time. All I thought about was that I was missing out on having fun. The risk of injury or rejection by my more physically adept peers never crossed my mind until the occasions when injury or rejection did occur because the restrictions imposed on me by my physical disability meant that I *was* unable to participate in certain activities.

To this day, I remain a proud and stubborn person, which makes it difficult for me to admit in writing that I am more physically vulnerable than, for example, my able-bodied twin brother. After all, I am a twice graduated, married man who has enjoyed nearly twenty-five-years as a professional journalist. In many respects, I believe that God has enabled me to enjoy more occupational and personal success than many people who do not have a disability. However, I must stop committing the sin of pride on this page, put on my big-boy pants, and state that having cerebral palsy does make me more vulnerable to physical injury when I am performing tasks that most non-disabled people complete without thinking about it. For example,

I struggle to maintain my balance when I walk. This is because the amount of strength in my legs is not comparable with an able-bodied person of my age. My inability to judge distance and speed makes crossing the road a difficult task. Those are but two realities I live with every day.

In the Bible, we read of several instances of people who became or, at the very least, felt more vulnerable by the onset of physical disability or mental illness. Let's look at the area of physical disability first, In Genesis 27, we read how Rebekah and Jacob took advantage of aging Isaac's blindness to trick the father into blessing Jacob with the firstborn son's due (v. 27–29.) Had Isaac's eyesight been good, his wife and younger son would have found it impossible to exploit him in that way. Isaac was certainly rendered vulnerable to deception by his visual disability, as it left him unable to recognise his two sons.

Turning to the subject of mental illness. Occurrences of psychological upset in any form can also leave a person feeling more vulnerable to circumstances and situations, including depression and thoughts of suicide. To be honest, I have endured several episodes of depression throughout my life, even being diagnosed in 2014 with an anxiety disorder. Subsequently, I have been able to access the medicinal and psychological services required to 'mind my head' more effectively and therefore experience less emotional trauma.

The impact that depression and other mental illnesses have on the sufferer and those who love them can range from annoying to paralyzing. These conditions must be thought of as just as immobilizing as any physical disability. Certainly, I am more vulnerable to negative thoughts during episodes of extreme anxiety than I am when my mind and emotions are on an even keel. For example, I have never wanted to die on account of the pain caused by cerebral palsy, but I have fantasized about ending my life during periods of severe anxiety because I have felt that if I were dead, the deep hurt that I am enduring in that moment would stop.

In 1 Kings 18, we read of the prophet Elijah's greatest moment, when God used him to defeat the prophets of Baal. However, this triumph is quickly followed in the next chapter when Elijah appears to fall into a deep depression as a result of Queen Jezebel's threats to his life. (19:2) Such is the impact of the prophet's depression that 'He came to a broom bush, sat down under it and prayed that he might die. "I have had enough, LORD," he said. "Take my life; I am no better than my ancestors"' (19:4).

Just like me, Elijah pleaded with the Lord to end his life, for he was at the end of his tether. Another prophet, Jonah, in Jonah 4:8, became so depressed and frustrated in the heat that he said to the Lord, 'It would be better for me to die than to live.'

What strikes me is that Elijah and Jonah were so emotionally low that they felt it would be better to end their earthly existence. In human terms, there is a feeling of hopelessness which leads to the conclusion that life is no longer worth living. The author of Ecclesiastes aptly said it this way: 'Life is useless, all is useless' (Eccl. 1:2).

Unfortunately for people with disabilities, being spoken about in ways in which they are made to feel 'useless' directly because of their conditions is far from unheard of.

From Bible times right up to the present day, a mind-set which, however unintentionally, labels disabled people as individuals who have limited worth or purpose is not uncommon.

As my working day ends and I tire again, go ahead and turn the page and reflect on the next mind-set.

CHAPTER EIGHT

'HE IS TWO YEARS BEHIND HIS BROTHER'

The Useless Mind-Set on Disability

When I was in primary school, a doctor visited me in my home. His job was to assess my physical and mental capabilities. This elderly gentleman possessed limited people skills and even less tact. At one point during a conversation with my mum, the doctor remarked, 'So Joseph would be about two years behind his brother, then.'

Though I presume that he meant me no harm by his utterance, it had a profound effect on me for years to come. From that day on, I thought of myself as somewhat less than other children my age. I came to believe that I was of no use or value in the real world.

My experience that day left me with a great sense of empathy for people like Mephibosheth, the son of Jonathan, who was 'lame in both feet' (2 Sam. 9:12), the two blind men whom Jesus met and healed (Matt. 20:29–34), and the ten lepers Jesus also healed (Luke 17:11–19).

Mephibosheth was left permanently disabled after falling or being dropped by his nurse (2 Sam. 4:4) as they attempted to flee to safety after hearing that Saul, Jonathan, and his brothers had died on Mount Gilboa (1 Sam. 31:1–6).

Many years later, after David had ascended to the throne of Israel, he enquired, 'Is there anyone still left of the house of Saul to whom I can show kindness for Jonathan's sake?' (2 Sam. 9:1). When he was informed about the existence of Jonathan's son, Mephibosheth, the king immediately arranged a place of honour for the stricken man at his personal dining table and the restoration of all his family property and with servants to tend to it (vv. 7–11.)

Mephibosheth's response showed his gratitude, but note his words: 'What is your servant, that you should notice a dead dog like me?' (v. 8). This indicates how society regarded Mephibosheth. In short, he was a crippled man who was of less importance than a dead animal because of his damaged feet.

Likewise with the lepers who had been driven outside of society to avoid infecting others with their illness. Not only were they regarded as 'other' in the sense of being different from the people who were free of leprosy, but also they were thought of as having little to no value because of the condition that blighted their skin. Essentially, they were banished to a scrapheap.

The clearest example of society branding disabled people as useless or unworthy is demonstrated by the attitude of the crowd towards two blind men who cried out to Jesus as He and His disciples made their way to Jericho (Matt. 20:29–34). Their plea, 'Lord, Son of David, have mercy on us' (v. 30), was initially met with a 'rebuke' from the assembled crowd, who ordered them to 'be quiet' (v. 31). In my view, the onlookers demanded this because they did not believe two unsighted beggars were worthy of Jesus's time.

However, impoverished blind men were not the only ones society regarded useless based on a disability. Let's revisit mighty Babylonian Emperor Nebuchadnezzar, whose 'greatness reached the sky' while his 'dominion extend[ed] to distant parts of the earth (Dan. 4:22). Twelve months after Daniel predicted the king's fall from grace, Nebuchadnezzar boasted of his glorious achievements, giving no credit to God, who had blessed him. The Lord's response was swift and decisive as he pronounced judgement on the arrogant earthly monarch. At a word from the true and living God, the emperor lost his kingdom, authority, and sanity.'Immediately what had been said about Nebuchadnezzar was fulfilled. He was driven away from people and ate grass like the ox. His body was drenched with the dew of heaven until his hair grew like the feathers of an eagle and his nails like the claws of a bird' (v. 33). A man who ruled over the known world of his day suffers an impairment and loses everything in a second. Worse still, he is sent away, condemned to live like cattle until such time that God restores his mental health.

Fast-forward to the early 1990s and you may get there just in time to see my fourteen-year-old self also being written off as I was pronounced 'slow to learn' and with intelligence deemed 'below normal' by a respected Consultant Paediatrician. Effectively, I too felt 'put out to pasture' by an authority greater than myself in the form of the medical profession!

On the reverse side, I have met many people who view those with disabilities as 'inspirational'. I believe them to be well-meaning, but this attitude creates unrealistic expectations for disabled people, which places an impractical burden on them which they are unable to live up to. At risk of sounding ungrateful to the many well-meaning people who have offered me encouragement over the years by ferociously extolling even the tiniest of my virtues, I ask you to flick over to the next page, which will begin to explain why being of a mind-set to flatter people with disabilities can actually impede their development by failing to maximise their genuine strengths and acknowledge weaknesses.

CHAPTER NINE

'YOU PUT OTHER PEOPLE TO SHAME'

The Flattering Mind-Set on Disability

Imagine, if you will, eating dinner in a restaurant and being interrupted by a stranger who is moved to tears by the way you successfully operate a knife and fork. Or you meet someone in the restaurant car park who, on witnessing our successful five-step journey to the car, rushes over to hail you as an 'inspiration' to them.

Several of my friends who are physically disabled and I have all experienced similar incidents. I have never heard anyone congratulate my able-bodied twin brother for making his way over the road, yet I am a hero in a stranger's eyes for doing this.

Viewing people with disabilities as heroic for simply living their lives is, in my view, unhelpful because it overlooks their flaws and minimizes their genuine strengths.

The most obvious example of this view in the Bible is revealed in the story of King David and Mephibosheth, the grandson of David's long-term adversary, Saul, and son of his best friend, Jonathan. As we've already discussed, Mephibosheth was lame, and he regarded himself as a dead dog. Because of King David's deep friendship with his father, Mephibosheth became an object of the king's kindness. David said to him, 'I will restore to you all the land that belonged to your grandfather Saul, and you will always eat at my table' (2 Sam. 9:7). What's more, David charged Saul's former servant, Ziba, and his sons with tending the land so that Mephibosheth's needs would always be met.

In light of Mephibosheth's limitations, David's generous and compassionate act of providing such physical support may have been necessary. That said, Saul's disabled grandson was certainly a man with physical and intellectual capacity. Mephibosheth was a father of a young son, Mika (v. 12), a clear indication that this man lived in ways that transcended many expectations of people with disabilities.

Several years later, we find the suggestion that Mephibosheth had betrayed King David's trust and was now waiting in Jerusalem for an impending revival of his grandfather's kingdom. Mephibosheth denies this allegation, claiming to have been betrayed by Ziba. His insistence that the servant should take all Saul's property in the wake of King David's safe return from battle indicates that Mephibosheth may have been telling the truth (16:3, 26–30). However, that Saul's disabled grandson would even for a moment be considered capable of participating in a plot to overthrow God's chosen ruler suggests that there was more to him than just his lame feet.

Earlier in the Old Testament, we are introduced to Abraham's son Isaac, who acquired a visual disability later in life: blindness (Gen. 27:1).

Isaac's wife, Rebekah, and his younger son, Jacob, took advantage of his blindness. To gain the blessing of the firstborn son, mother and son concocted a plan to trick Isaac into thinking that Jacob was really his older brother, Esau. It worked! Jacob received the blessing that belonged to his brother. (See Gen. 27:5–14, 35.) Because of Isaac's blindness, his terrible error not only tore apart his family but also spawned the Edomites, born out of Esau's willingness to marry foreign women (vv. 42–47), who became an enemy nation to Israel.

Isaac was a notable character in the Old Testament. This position in life was a wonderful reflection of God's blessings on him; however, to view this physically impaired man as purely inspirational is to overlook his character flaws.

God has used me and my physical circumstances to advance His kingdom. That said, I am reluctant to be described as inspirational because I am aware of my many human weaknesses. These limitations mean that while God has graciously used various aspects of my life, including my disability, to bring glory to His name, my witness to His grace is imperfect. I am determined that I will continue to strive with the Lord until my life on earth is over.

Many people with disabilities, myself included, have been described as having a determined mind-set when it comes to living our lives. By this, our encouragers mean that we are exceptionally keen that our attitude is such that we do not permit our conditions to get in the way of living what they describe as a 'normal' life—one which is full of activities, achievements, and goals that are on a par with what they, non-disabled people, have accomplished.

Life experience has taught me that if you have a disability, a considerable degree of extra determination is needed to succeed in life. There are two reasons for this. Firstly, the restrictions placed on a person as a direct result of disability may mean that a task is physically, intellectually, or emotionally harder to complete than it would be for a non-disabled person. Secondly, is it sometimes the case that the people who are part of the disabled person's life may, often unintentionally, make it harder for him or her to achieve a task or goal by discouraging him or her from working towards it. Often, this happens with the best of intentions. For example, those who love the disabled person may discourage them from working towards a goal because they fear that failure to achieve it will leave their loved one feeling disheartened.

However, if you are a disabled person and wish to achieve a long-held dream, you may need to find the strength to ignore well-meaning naysayers and press on towards your cherished ambition. This attitude is best described as a determined mind-set. Come with me now as I ignore an irritating back spasm and reflect on this mind-set.

CHAPTER TEN

'HAVING A DISABILITY WON'T STOP ME'

The Determined Mind-Set

I rarely find writing to be a difficult task. In fact, I thoroughly enjoy every second of my work. However, I once had real problems as I tried to ghost-write the biography of an athlete with spina bifida who had refused to be limited by his disability. He left his bedridden state, worked and trained to successfully compete in a marathon, and eventually became a personal trainer.

The difficulty I encountered was that this man was adamant that his disability was not to be referred to in his biography. He had been raised with the mind-set that walking with crutches or being in a wheelchair did not make him any less capable of living a 'normal' life. This was the case to such an extent that he believed that spina bifida had played no part in his life at any point.

His bedridden years were, according to him, the result of a venomous dog bite he had received as a teenager coupled with 'bad food choices', leading to weight gain over the years and subsequent immobility.

You may or may not agree with his attitude of living with a disability. I admire his determination. Whilst I agree that is it possible to have a rich and fulfilling life with a disability, my personal experiences—the physical, social, and emotional consequences of having a notable condition—teach me that my life differs from my non-disabled twin.

There are, however, examples in God's Word of people whose disability did not impact their ability to do outstanding things, even to the point that their impairment is rarely mentioned, except to say that it existed.

Take Ehud, for example, who delivered the disobedient Israelite nation from tyranny at the hand of Eglon, king of Moab. Ehud was a descendant of Benjamin, a tribe whose members had the gift ambidexterity, which enabled them to 'shoot arrows or to sling stones right-handed or left-handed' (I Chron. 12:2). Not so Ehud, who was 'a left-handed man', thereby being different from other members of this family in that he was less able to use his right side. However, God used the deliverer's one-sidedness to His advantage to slay the tyrannical Eglon and defeat Moab.

Ehud brought to Eglon a present from the people of Israel. But that's not all he planned to give to the king. 'Now Ehud had made a double-edged sword about a cubit long, which he strapped to his right thigh under his clothing'. Eglon is described as 'a very fat man'. Once Ehud had given the king the gift, he informed the king that he had 'a message from God' for him. That was enough to persuade the monarch to order his attendants to leave, enabling Ehud to pull out the sword with his left hand and plunge it into the king's overgrown belly before he realized what was happening. Eglon was dead before his servants found him, rendering the Moabites leaderless and fearful. Indeed, in a remarkable turnaround, 'Moab was made subject to Israel, and the land had peace for eighty years.' (See Judg. 3:12–30.)

Ehud's disability was certainly not, according to my reading of the passage, recorded as a 'problem'; rather, it made his task of releasing Israel from dictatorship easier.

Likewise, the 'wrenching' of Jacob's hip after as he wrestled with the angel of God (Gen. 32:25), and its physical impact, does not appear to play a part in the rest of his life or his achievements for the kingdom. In fact, grappling with and surviving wrestling with God led to Jacob's being honoured with a new name: *Israel* (v. 28).

Living with a disability as the world defines it cannot be completely ignored. However, the circumstances arising from it can, with a determined mind-set, be used to bring glory to God and help others. For me, that is one facet of the 'life to the full' (John 10:10) as it applies to Christians who are differently abled and willing to be used by Jesus for the Saviour's perfect purposes.

In my view, it is only by adopting what I describe as Christ's mind-set on disability that it is possible to reach one's maximum potential.

CHAPTER ELEVEN

'GO AND TELL OF WHAT THE LORD HAS DONE FOR YOU'

Christ's Mind-Set on Disability

As with all things, God, in the person of his Son, Jesus Christ, displayed while He was here on earth the perfect attitude towards people who have disabilities or illnesses. His dealings with individuals in this position were characterised by four admirable attributes

Jesus Treated People with Disabilities as Individuals

One of the first things I noticed as I read the accounts of how Jesus interacted with people who had disabilities or illnesses was the way in which He recognised their individuality and humanity. No two people with impairments were the same to Jesus. For example, the woman who had endured severe bleeding for twelve years received healing simply by touching Jesus's cloak (Luke 8:44).

Bartimaeus, who was blind, received his sight after the Saviour spoke, 'Go, your faith has healed you' (Mark 10:52). Another man, also blind, was granted the ability to see after he went into the pool of Siloam and washed away the mud that Jesus had placed in his eyes (John 9:11). Through the prophet Elisha, God told Naaman to 'wash seven times in the River Jordan' to be healed of his leprosy (2 Kings 5:10). Jesus healed ten men with leprosy by commanding them to '"Go, show yourselves to the priests." And as they went, they were cleansed' (Luke 17:14).

One of the ten men who received healing returned to Jesus and 'threw himself at Jesus' feet and thanked him.' Jesus responded to this one man. 'Rise and go; your faith has made you well' (Luke 17:18–19). What a contrast to this man's previous existence as part of a seemingly homogenous group of skin-diseased men. He received an individual vindication from the King of Kings! Although the passage ends there, I can imagine that Christ's words only added to his sense of joy and self-worth. I suggest this because I have been at my most inspired and productive when people have recognised me as Joe, a great journalist, or something other than 'the handicapped fella.'

Jesus Treated People Who Had Disabilities with Genuine Respect and Kindness

On a similar note, Jesus treated the disabled people He met not only as individuals but also with kindness and respect. He authentically loved them without patronising them. The 'trembling' woman who faced Jesus after she was healed of long-term blood loss was greeted as a 'Daughter' by Christ (Luke 8:48).

Likewise, Jesus overruled the assembled crowd who 'rebuked [Bartimaeus] and told him to be quiet' (Mark 10:48). Unflustered by popular expectation, Jesus called for the blind man to be brought into His presence and asked him those memorable words which kicked off a life-changing sequence of events.

'What do you want me to do for you?' Jesus asked him.

The blind man said, 'Rabbi, I want to see.'

'"Go," said Jesus, "your faith has healed you." Immediately he received his sight and followed Jesus along the road' (vv. 51–52).

This miracle is told in just four verses. This indicates that the first encounter between Jesus and Bartimaeus was a short one in which a brief act of kindness literally brought light to a person's world.

Jesus Met Not Only the Medical Needs of Those with Disabilities but Also Their Wider Spiritual Ones

In Mark 2:1–12, we read the account of Jesus healing a man who was fully paralysed so that all he could do was lie on a mat. The man's friends were determined that he should meet Jesus. However, getting this man through the packed crowd was nearly impossible. Undaunted, they carried the man to the top of the house where Jesus was staying. They then cut a hole in the roof and lowered the man on his stretcher through it and bringing him to rest on the floor in front of Jesus. Jesus immediately healed the man of his paralysis when He commanded him to 'get up, take your mat and go home' (v. 11). The next verse reveals that the assembled audience were 'amazed' when they saw this previously bedbound man get up and walk out. Indeed, the writer notes: 'They praised God, saying, "We have never seen anything like this!"'

Impressive as the healing was, I believe that the most significant words spoken by Jesus during the encounter are found in Matthew's account. The gospel writer makes a particularly striking point. 'Some men brought to him a paralyzed man, lying on a mat. When Jesus saw their faith, He said to the man, "Take heart, son; your sins are forgiven"' (Matt. 9:2). Jesus was profoundly aware of the man's difficult situation on earth, and He did not make light of it. However, He recognised that the condition of the man's soul was also at stake. Aware that He alone was 'the way, the truth and the life' and that no one could come to the Father except through Him (John 14:6), the Saviour wasted no time in ensuring that the patient's sins were forgiven. Heaven was the man's ultimate destiny, much to the dismay of the watching 'teachers of the law' (Mark 2:6).

I was fortunate enough to have been taught the gospel message from an early age. As part of this, I was told that my earthly situation is temporary, but my soul will live forever in either heaven or hell, depending solely on how I responded to Jesus's offer of salvation. If I accepted Jesus as my Saviour, my sins would be forgiven, and I would go to a place where '"He will wipe every tear from their eyes. There will be no more death" or mourning or crying or pain, for the old order of things has passed away' (Rev. 21:4). However, if I rejected Christ, my name would not be 'written in the book of life' and I would spend eternity 'in the lake of fire' (20:15). The paralysed man faced this same choice, as does anyone with or without a disability. Our greatest need is to have a personal relationship with Jesus Christ.

Jesus Commissioned People with Disabilities to Serve in His Kingdom

In Acts 9:8, we read that Paul 'could see nothing' when he got to his feet after he heard the voice of

Jesus for the first time on the road to Damascus. Jesus commissioned the visually disabled, soon-to-be apostle with the words, 'Now get up and go into the city, and you will be told what you must do' (v. 6). With that one sentence spoken by Jesus, a blind man began a journey that would spread the gospel throughout Europe to the heretofore unreached gentiles. (See Gal: 1:15–16.)

Later in God's Word, we hear of Timothy, a young evangelist who is beset with stomach problems. Such is the extent of his trouble that the apostle Paul advised him to 'Stop drinking only water, and use a little wine because of your stomach and your frequent illnesses' (1 Tim. 5:23). Meanwhile, in 2 Corinthians 12:7, Paul reveals that he also suffered from 'a painful physical ailment.'

Zacchaeus, a tax-collector who was, it seems, afflicted with a form of dwarfism (Luke 19:3) is an example of someone whom Jesus was keen to invite into His kingdom. After Jesus 'came to stay' (v. 5) at his house one afternoon, the repentant sinner made the following pledge to his newfound Saviour: 'Look, Lord! Here and now I give half of my possessions to the poor, and if I have cheated anybody out of anything, I will pay back four times the amount' (19:8).

In response to Zacchaeus's act of honesty, Christ declared: 'Today salvation has come to this house, because this man, too, is a son of Abraham.

For the Son of Man came to seek and to save the lost' (v. 9).

What a trio of testimonies to lives changed by the love of Jesus! Illness or physical disability was no barrier to Paul, Timothy, or Zacchaeus to be used by God to build His kingdom. Neither is it to me or anyone else.

Notice that in contrast to the world's attitudes towards people with disabilities, Christ did not treat them as one group with universal needs, nor was He ashamed of or embarrassed by them. Equally, Jesus was not crippled with sentimental pity. I do not find any instances when the Lord hailed disabled people as inspiring simply on the basis that they lived their lives. Instead, He loved people with disabilities as people, and He focused on their strengths when presenting them with a challenging commission to work for His kingdom.

God can use disability and the circumstances it creates to improve and bring about positive change in the world while drawing others closer to Him. Each person has a specific role in Christ's service, even if 'the world' writes them off because they are 'disabled.' The key to fulfilling your God-given destiny is to submit your heart and your life fully to the Saviour and ask Him to use every aspect of yourself for His glory. My personal testimony from 'retarded' toddler to double-graduate journalist who has produced faith-centred articles for the past twenty-five years is proof of His power to change an apparently hopeless prognosis for the good. The God who brought about this remarkable turnaround in my life can also do it for you if you place your trust fully in Him.

If it is the case that God can and does act within the people with disabilities in the extension of His Kingdom, the question we must then ask is, Should we dream of or expect a cure for any and all disabilities or illnesses we have now or will develop in the future? What does the Bible say about this? My eyes are closing as I again crave rest. I will leave you to cast your eyes over the next few pages, which consider these questions while I grab another nap.

CHAPTER TWELVE

'WILL YOU EVER GET BETTER?'

The Biblical Perspective on Healing

What is the biblical view on the curing or healing those affected by disability?

The subject of cures for disabilities and illness and what the Bible says about this is not controversial. The same cannot be said for the many, often flawed, interpretations that people take out of what they read. For that reason, an ill-judged answer to the question posed in the title of this chapter is likely either to cause offence or to give false hope to people whose lives are impacted by sickness or disability.

Throughout this book, I have highlighted several incidents of miraculous healings Jesus performed while here on earth. As a committed Christian, I believe that everything written in the

Bible is true. One such truth is found in Hebrews 13:8: 'Jesus Christ is the same yesterday and today and forever.'

On the strength of this verse, I have heard many people ask, 'Why does God continue to allow people to endure disability and illness? One word from Him and every sickness under the sun would be healed.'

Many people whom I believe are soundly saved brothers and sisters in the family of God quote the portion of Isaiah 53:5, which says, 'by his wounds we are healed' as a basis for believing that universal healing is available to everyone while they are here on earth. I believe that people who use the verse in this context are sincere and motivated by love; however, this verse must be read in the context of the whole chapter. The passage foretells the coming of Jesus as the Messiah, who would come to take the punishment for humankind's sin. Whoever believes in Him will enjoy eternal life with God in heaven when their time in this broken world is over (see John 3:16). Jesus was indeed 'pierced for our transgressions, he *was* crushed for our iniquities; the punishment that brought us peace *was* on him, and by His wounds we *are* healed' (Isa. 53:5, emphasis mine).

However, rather than universal healing, this verse refers to spiritual and eternal healing. This is a prophecy of the Messiah's death on the cross so that sinful humankind could be drawn back into a relationship with Him.

Verse 4 of the same chapter says: 'Surely he took up our pain and bore our sorrows, yet we considered him punished by God, stricken by him, and afflicted.' This is further indication that when God's Word talks about universal healing, it is referring to spiritual restoration between the Lord and human beings, not physical healing as many people define it.

Additional evidence that the Bible does not promise complete healing for everyone this side of eternity is the reflections of the apostle Paul in 2 Corinthians 12. Here he recalls being 'caught up' (v. 2) in what appears to have been a vision of heaven where he saw 'inexpressible things' (v. 4). Paul was given 'a thorn in [his] flesh' (v. 7) to prevent him from becoming filled with pride at what he had seen. The apostle is honest enough to admit that three times he had asked God to take the ailment away (v. 8) but that Lord had told him, 'My grace is sufficient for you, for my power is made perfect in weakness' (v. 9). Based on my understanding of the Bible and my personal experience, God works through life situations, including disability and illness, to both increase a person's faith in Him and extend His kingdom.

I would suggest that the notable healings of Jesus and the works of others on behalf of the kingdom were carried out not primarily as a means of relieving suffering but to demonstrate God's divine power and authority. Remember the paralysed man I referred to in the previous chapter? Jesus's first act was to forgive his sins (Matt. 9:2; Mark 2:2). When the teachers of the law accused Jesus of blasphemy (v. 3; v. 7, respectively), His command to the paralysed man to get up demonstrated His authority not only to forgive sins but also to do much more.

That is not to say that Jesus did not act out of mercy to heal someone. For example, in Matthew 12:9–14 we read that Jesus spoke healing over a man with a withered hand to teach that showing mercy was more important to Him than keeping rigid laws. In the main, however, Jesus and His apostles used healing, first and foremost, to demonstrate Christ's power and authority.

Acts 3 recalls the episode when Peter and John, two of the Lord's disciples, encountered a lame man as they went to pray at the temple close to the Beautiful Gate one afternoon. Spotting the man, they commanded him to 'look at us' (v. 4). We are told the man looked, expecting to be given money. His life was changed in a much more lasting way when Peter uttered the mind-blowing words, 'Silver and gold I do not have, but what I do have I give you. In the name of Jesus Christ of Nazareth, walk' (v. 6).

In a nutshell, the subsequent verses tell us that when Peter helped the man to his feet, the disability vanished instantly from his limbs. He jumped, leapt, and praised God, while the people who witnessed the recovery were filled with awe because of what they had witnessed.

The healing of the lame man by Peter and John through the name of Jesus does, I believe, illustrate another very important point: God's willingness to use people to invoke healing in others. First Corinthians 12:9 says that some people have the gift of healing, a fact which justifies and, indeed, encourages the use of doctors and other medical professionals to bring about wellness in human beings. All such attributes are gifts of the Spirit given to those within the body of Christ to the extension of His glory.

Many Christians whom I admire greatly have reported witnessing healing as a result of prayer. These miracles are not to be downplayed or denied; rather, when they occur, it is a demonstration of God's authority, not a confirmation of physical healing for everyone.

On a significant number of occasions when I have gathered with others to pray for the relief of illness, God has answered by taking the person being prayed for to be with Him in heaven. This is where, according to Revelation 21:3–5, He will 'dwell' with them, make 'everything new!' '"He will wipe every tear from their eyes. There will be no more death" or mourning or crying or pain, for the old order of things has passed away.' Any pain or discomfort caused by disability will be gone. That is the healing that Jesus won for everyone who trusts Him as Saviour.

I am certain that we will have difficulties in this life. For some that may include a disability. But 2 Corinthians 4:17–18 says, ' For our light and momentary troubles are achieving for us an eternal glory that far outweighs them all. So we fix our eyes not on what is seen, but on what is unseen, since what is seen is temporary, but what is unseen is eternal.'

I am the last person who will ever make light of the impact of pain. Like Paul, I have asked the Lord to remove my personal 'thorn.' That it will happen in heaven I am certain of. Until then, I know that, in common with everyone else, I am 'God's handiwork, created in Christ Jesus to do good works, which God prepared in advance for us to do' (Eph. 2:10).

I will admit that much of what I have written portrays disability and its impact in mostly a negative way. For that I will offer at least a partial apology because I believe with all my heart that God's Word offers clear guidance and instruction on how Christians who have a disability or illness are called to live meaningful, productive, and blessed lives.

It's time to unpack how this can be achieved.

CHAPTER THIRTEEN

'A CRIP AND A CHRISTIAN'

Living with the Correct Mind-Set

The starting point for living a Christ-centred life when you have a disability is to fully accept the truth that the devil as well as proud, sinful humankind are the causes of your impairment. Sin and all its consequences, including physical, intellectual and emotional impairment, entered the world when Adam and Eve believed the Father of Lies, Satan, rather than God. Neither I nor anyone else with a disability has the right to blame God for my condition.

Equally, I cannot use my physical state as a reason to reject Christ's offer of salvation and live a deliberately sinful life. My mind and power of rational thought are not impaired by my physical condition; therefore, I may not, unlike children and adults with severe learning disabilities, be spared a lost eternity unless I submit to Jesus as my Lord and Saviour. As a result, it is no more or less challenging for me to live for the Messiah than it is for someone who is able-bodied.

Indeed, I believe Jesus's promise of 'life—life in all its fullness' (John 10:10 GNT) provides me with added incentive to live for Him. Without God's power in my life to help me negotiate painful days and ensure each one counts for my good and His eternal kingdom, my earthly existence is simply a tale of pain, restriction, and limitation. I would perhaps have a few good moments on account of the 'common grace' and blessing that the loving Creator God allows most people to enjoy. Without God, a life spent with a condition which, on the face of it, causes soreness and limitation would be a very hard existence. However, with the loving and all-powerful God in my corner, my life matters. The same is, of course, true of every life, because God is the Creator of all people. However, because I am a Christian, He has given me extra reasons to live. God has given me gifts, blessings, and abilities that have been developed by the experiences, people, and situations I have encountered *because* I have cerebral palsy.

Add an eternal dimension to my faith in Christ, and you will get an even clearer picture of why I am happy to follow God, CP and all. The promises in the early verses of Revelation 21 say it all. I have a place waiting for me in the 'new heaven and the new earth' where there will be no more tears, mourning, crying, or pain. I am convinced that even if my life on earth were devoid of any form of blessing, what awaits me in heaven would more than make up for any temporary pain.

I praise God now and always for the ability to succeed in the tasks He allows me to do each day. To be honest, the level of pain I have experienced during the compilation of this book has been at the highest and most consistent level I have experienced outside of post-operative situations. On most days, my padded chair has provided little protection from bursts of agony. At risk of trotting out a Bible-based cliché, I can do all the things I do only 'through Christ who strengthens me' (Phil. 4:13 NKJV), in truth, I couldn't rise from my bed in the morning unless I cried (sometimes literally) to God, who gives me the strength to do it. Prayers continue throughout the day for the ability to perform what some people might think of as simple tasks like walking to the kitchen and getting something to eat, or getting safely wherever I need to go. As for the ability to write a book or produce content for a daily news website, that requires prayer on another level!

I also believe that regularly and methodically reading God's Word is crucial for any Christian, especially those who have a disability. Only by reading the Word and allowing His glorious promises to become deeply ingrained in your mind will you find the strength to keep going during those times when the pain, restriction, or limits you endure become too much. I have been blessed to find answers to the problems I encounter with CP throughout day-to-day living simply through reading the Bible.

I have also been blessed with a wonderful Christian wife, family, and friends, whom God has sent to me as I walk with Him through this life. Even little Yogi is a great therapy dog! I pray I am a blessing to them as they are to me.

Don't fall into the trap of shutting yourself indoors. Instead, get out there, live, love, and enjoy the life God has given you. You have been born for a purpose. Discover what your gifts are and use them to the max for God. Blessing will follow.

Remember, too, that the promises of God given to those who seek Him are not diminished even if you have a condition that leads you to be physically or intellectually restricted in the eyes of the world. Paul spends a lot of time in Romans explaining that no one who confesses Jesus as Saviour will be excluded from the blessings and responsibilities associated with following Christ. His thoughts are summarised perfectly here:

> If you declare with your mouth, 'Jesus is Lord,' and believe in your heart that God raised him from the dead, you will be saved. For it is with your heart that you believe and are justified,

> and it is with your mouth that you profess your faith and are saved. As Scripture says, 'Anyone who believes in him will never be put to shame.' For there is no difference between Jew and Gentile—the same Lord is Lord of all and richly blesses all who call on him, for, 'Everyone who calls on the name of the Lord will be saved.' (10:9–13)

All of this from a man who, by his own admission, had once travelled on the road to Damascus, intending to put into prison anyone who preached this message (Acts 22:4). Along the way, Jesus Himself intervened in an incredible way to change Paul's mind-set and the course of His life forever.

Equally, in Acts 10:28 we find the apostle Peter admitting, 'God has shown me that I should not call anyone impure or unclean.' This was in stark contrast to his previous legalistic view that Jews and gentiles should not associate with one another.

I am convinced that the writings of both of these early Christian leaders demonstrate that disability is no barrier to being part of Christ's kingdom and the blessings therein.

God made all humans 'in His own image' (Gen. 1:27). That includes those with disabilities. People, disabled or not, bear God's image. Going deeper, in Psalm 139:4, we find David praising the Lord in the full knowledge that he is 'fearfully and wonderfully made.'

The Bible is the completely true, divinely inspired Word of God, with the implication that the words it contains are for everyone at all times and in all places. Remember, too, that God is flawless—He makes no mistakes. The prophet reveals that 'As for God, his way is perfect; the word of the LORD is tried: he is a buckler to all them that trust in him' (2 Sam. 22:31 KJV).

People with disabilities are not 'defective goods' sent from a heavenly body factory by a doddery grandfather who wrings his hands at broken machinery. Disability occurs as a result of fallen creation. But God is ever- and all-powerful, and no matter how tough situations may seem, we have the assurance that He will not allow anyone to be tested beyond what he or she is able to withstand (1 Cor. 10:13)

In short, a person with a disability is wonderfully made in God's own image by the Creator, who is incapable of error and compassionate to ensure that the struggles we may face need not overwhelm us. I reckon that considering this, I, along with everyone else who is 'differently able', have some serious responsibilities to fulfil.

Firstly, fellow believers in positions similar to my own and I are called to live in a way that manifests Galatians 5:22–23: 'the fruit of the spirit'. This means that our individual characters must display 'love, joy, peace, forbearance, kindness, goodness, faithfulness, gentleness and self-control'—even when our bodies are aching and our brains are playing tricks.

'But, Joe, my legs are aching. I haven't slept for a week. And last night I left a puddle on the floor en route to the toilet. What you are saying is nice in theory, but it is easier said than done.'

I hear you and fully agree. God understands that we will not live in perfect obedience to His will this side of eternity; hence, we have our 'advocate with the Father—Jesus Christ, the Righteous One' to plead for us (1 John 2:1). However, I truly believe that we who have physical struggles can make progress in our walk with God by donning His spiritual armour.

> Therefore put on the full armour of God, so that when the day of evil comes, you may be able to stand your ground, and after you have done everything, to stand. Stand firm then, with the belt of truth buckled around your waist, with the breastplate of righteousness in place, and with your feet fitted with the readiness that comes from the gospel of peace. In addition to all this, take up the shield of faith, with which you can extinguish all the flaming arrows of the evil one. Take the helmet of

> salvation and the sword of the Spirit, which is the word of God.
>
> And pray in the Spirit on all occasions with all kinds of prayers and requests. With this in mind, be alert and always keep on praying for all the Lord's people. (Ephesians 6:13–18)

Quite rightly, this passage begins by pointing out that 'our struggle is not against flesh and blood, but against the rulers, against the authorities, against the powers of this dark world and against the spiritual forces of evil in the heavenly realms' (v. 12). Disability and suffering are definitely the work of the devil ('powers of this dark world'), but it is, I believe, possible to defend oneself using the 'belt of truth' (v. 14).

Very simply, remember the promises God has made to you in His Holy Word. You are made in His image. You are not a mistake; rather, He created you for a life of good works, which He ordained specific ones for you, and only you, to complete in your present physical state and, perhaps, using the experiences you have gained because of the life circumstances it produces. For example, I was part of the fight in my hometown to ensure that the local mainstream college was made accessible to people with disabilities. I did this because my enrolment request was rejected due to my physical limitations. I didn't want others to be kept out of school because the building could not accommodate those with disabilities.

The 'breastplate of righteousness' refers to the knowledge that our existence on this earth and eternal salvation are validated by God. When the demon of low self-esteem attacks, remember that you are a part of 'the world' that God loved enough to send His Son, Jesus, to die for (John 3:16). If you are important enough that Christ died for you, then you can join Him in audibly telling Satan to 'get behind me' (Matt. 16:23). You are God's child, the son or daughter of the King of Kings. No one and nothing can change that, so focus on that truth and your place in God's affections.

In thinking about 'the shoes fitted with the gospel of peace' (v. 16), one of the biggest problems those of us with disabilities face is the internal battle to be 'as good as' our able-bodied peers. I have been guilty of trying to perform physically and cognitively at the same level as people who do not have a disability. Often, I have experienced extreme exhaustion coupled with crushing feelings of inferiority when I have failed to attain the same goals as everyone else. This attitude is, I believe, in direct disobedience to God's Word, which says: 'Do not conform to the pattern of this world, but be transformed by the renewing of your mind. Then you will be able to test and approve what God's will is—his good, pleasing and perfect will' (Rom. 12:2). In other words, God has assured us that He has a unique purpose for each of us. When we try to sidestep or go beyond that purpose for something we think is better, we lose inner contentment. As we say in Northern Ireland, 'Give your head peace.' Of course, living with an authentic sense of peace is impossible without putting up the 'shield of faith' (Eph. 6:16) and believing utterly the promises of God for our lives.

I know as well as anyone that maintaining a measure of faith upon waking in the morning with every bone in your body aching is hard. Sometimes that belief in the Lord's purposes for my life is barely as small 'as a mustard seed' (Luke 17:6). At times like that, I must keep the faith by praying to God in the Spirit, remembering that my prayers do not need to be refined by clever words or long sentences. Romans 8:26 tells us: 'In the same way, the Spirit helps us in our weakness. We do not know what we ought to pray for, but the Spirit himself intercedes for us through wordless groans.'

In my experience, it helps to pray simply for what I need. If I need strength to get out of bed, I pray for the strength to put my feet on the floor, to stand up, and then to move. 'The prayer of a righteous person is powerful and effective' (James 5:16) reminds me that I am made righteous through Jesus's sacrificial death on the cross, and the consequence of my prayers is power. Many times, my shield of faith is fortified by communication with God. I find that Satan's 'flaming arrows' dampen in the presence of God, while the 'sword of the Spirit,' which is God's Word, provides the knowledge and encouragement I need to understand that God is at work in my life, even in the toughest moments. I know that He will work in me as He did in Isaac, Paul, Jacob, and the other biblical figures we have met in this book.

I would be lying if I said that continuing with God while living with the pressures a disability brings is easy. There have been times in my faith journey when I have felt like yelling, 'What are You doing, God? Why are You taking such a long time to answer me?'

When I have felt like this, three verses of Scripture have helped me to keep trusting God. Firstly, I remember what Jesus said: 'Are not two sparrows sold for a penny? Yet not one of them will fall to the ground outside your Father's care' (Matt. 10:29). If God watches over sparrows so closely at all times, I believe that His attention to the needs of humanity is surely greater.

Secondly, Isaiah 65:4 reminds me that the Lord always answers prayer. 'Before they call I will answer; while they are still speaking I will hear.' God is never passive; He is always at work for the good of those He loves. The timings of His interventions are sometimes hard to understand, but every move God makes on our behalf is perfect for His purposes as well as our good. As with anything worthwhile, persistence is key to maintaining a relationship with God.

Lastly, I recall the verses which suggest that faith is strengthened through hardship. 'Not only so, but we also glory in our sufferings, because we know that suffering produces perseverance; perseverance, character; and character, hope. And hope does not put us to shame, because God's love has been poured out into our hearts through the Holy Spirit, who has been given to us' (Rom. 5:3–5). Perhaps you understand when I say that at times when I have felt physically sore or mentally low, the first person I cry to is God. After all, He created me, He knows my every thought, and He is the only One who can really pull me through.

What's more, just as He told the struggling apostle, I also have God's personal assurance: '"My grace is sufficient for you, for my power is made perfect in weakness." Therefore I will boast all the more gladly about my weaknesses, so that Christ's power may rest on me' (2 Cor. 12:9). Looking back through the lens of this verse, I can now see that it was because I had a visible weakness that God used me to instigate the local educational facilities to make their buildings accessible to disabled people.

One result of my disability is that I am compelled to search the Word to bring a message of hope to those who are in a similar position as I am, as well as to people who provided care and support. Days of pain, frustration, and disappointment, consequences of my cerebral palsy on my brain and body, have, by a strange paradox, given me an unshakable joy, the culmination of which is the 'helmet of salvation'. I am God's child. I am saved to live for Him here on earth doing what only I can do for Him before ruling forever in victory with our risen Christ in heaven.

Hallelujah! Let it be, or simply: Amen.

AFTERWORD

Keeping It 'Real Real Real'

It's 10.38 a.m. on 27 September 2019, five months and six days since I started researching and writing *Trading Mind-Sets: Faith, God, and Disability.* Quelle surprise, you find me sitting in the same swivel chair, typing one fingered on my trusty Lenovo.

Happily, the hinge joint in my knee is less painful than it was a few months ago, thanks to receiving a good stretch at the gym yesterday. My spine remains more comfortable in flexion than when it is straight, and my head is thinking about a leisurely breakfast and a catch-up with the newspapers as a reward for this morning's exertions.

Compiling this manuscript has been, without a doubt, the most challenging piece of writing I have undertaken in my career to date. I say this because the subject of disability, what it means and how it is regarded, is a much more complex topic that I had first envisaged. As for the question of whether healing is possible or to be expected, or whether a person can live positively with a disability, let's just say that I endured brain freeze on more than a few occasions as I tried to unpack what I believe God wanted to say to me about these issues. A lie-in is most definitely required tomorrow, I think!

Before I finally rest, I want to remind you about the objectives I set at the outset of this book.

Firstly, I presented what the Bible says about the causes of disability and illness. I also examined some of the different, but sometimes overlapping, mind-sets on disability found in the Bible, including Christ's, which He displayed during His time on earth. Thirdly, I unpacked the biblical position on the healing and curing of disabilities, including whether this is to be expected today. Finally, with a lot of help from God through His Scripture, I offered encouragement to those who live with some form of disability.

I used the narrative in Genesis 2 to demonstrate that God created a wonderful, colourful, and vibrant world, which He blessed and pronounced everything He'd made was good. If Adam and Eve had followed the Lord's instruction and not eaten fruit from the forbidden tree, then disability, with all the pain, limitations, and trials that go along with it, would not exist. It is as simple as that. God, as revealed to us in human form as Jesus Christ, was the perfect, spotless One, without sin (1 Peter 2:22; 2 Cor. 5:21). He had no desire or inclination to make a single person feel a second of pain. Human beings went their own way, and the consequences include that our bodies will fail.

My scribblings offer only brief insight into the way in which people with disabilities and illnesses were regarded in the Bible. Using various examples from Scripture, we encountered a range of mind-sets: shame, vulnerability, and rejection of individuality. We saw attitudes towards disabled people stretching from their being of little use or value or to the other extreme of being inspirational or heroic but in the inflated and unhelpful sense. People with disabilities can, in some cases, fall into mind-sets of self-pity or self-loathing, or believe that disability has no real impact on their lives or outlook.

Jesus demonstrated the perfect attitude towards disabled people. He healed many of those of their disabilities, such as blind Bartimaeus, ten men with leprosy, and a man who was fully paralysed and had to be carried around on his mat. These are but three of numerous people Jesus healed. The healing and care He offered went hand in hand with an instruction to go and live the gospel, telling others of what God had done for them. The Lord challenged disabled people to labour with others in His kingdom, thereby affirming their worth as individuals. But most of all, Jesus recognised that their greatest need was to know spiritual freedom in the form of sins forgiven.

By showing mercy to these people, Jesus demonstrated compassion and respect for those with disabilities. He affirmed their worth and purpose for His kingdom. By implication, we are to have the same attitude towards them and others who are struggling. Going further, I believe that God does not regard disabled people as objects of pity to be simply looked after. Jacob, who was left with a walking impairment after wrestling with God, was given the task of building arguably the most significant dynasty in Israel's history. The apostle Paul was afflicted with a thorn in his flesh, yet God chose him to introduce the gospel into what would become Europe. In human terms, people living in my home continent have his determination and courage to thank for our faith.

God is the same yesterday, today, and forever; therefore, He can heal today as He did in biblical times. However, God's Word suggests that the healings Jesus did and those done subsequently by His apostles were performed as demonstrations of God's power, mercy, and authority. Many of the verses in the Bible regarding healing are referring to spiritual restoration. In a nutshell, through Jesus's death on the cross and His resurrection three days later, people can know spiritual restoration, receive forgiveness of sin, and enjoy eternal life in heaven, where all will experience full physical and intellectual healing and be free from suffering, pain, and death.

Christians, such as the apostle Paul, testified that God used their form of disability for His glory as well as for their emotional and spiritual well-being.

I hope I have helped you to understand that because God is not the author of disability, a Christian, or indeed anyone with any form of impairment, cannot live in a way that blames the Lord for the issues they face. One must, I suggest, take hold of the many promises that God has for His followers, safe in the knowledge that these apply to Christians who have a disability just as much as those who are able-bodied. Putting on the full armour of God will help you to do this.

Read His Word each day, talk to Him and other trusted Christian friends about how you are feeling. If upon awakening in the morning you are able to only open your eyes, praise God for that and ask for His strength to do more. This takes practice and commitment. Honestly, it is a lifelong process. The reward is, in my experience, a sense of joy like no other. When times get hard, remember that all the promises that God made to His followers, including 'life—and life in all its fullness' while you are here on earth and in your heavenly home, are as much for people with disability as they are for other members of God's family. Believe, trust God, communicate with Him constantly, asking for what you need, and you will receive it. You may not get what you think you want, nor will help always come in the way you expect, but exactly what you need when you need it will arrive. God is all-powerful, He is not a liar, and He never fails.

Allow me to recall the words of Gaelic sporting legend Mickey Harte, whose daughter, Michaela McAreavey, was cruelly murdered on her honeymoon to Mauritius in 2011. When asked during a Q and A at my local Town Hall how he had managed to go on in the wake of his daughter's death, he replied, 'The success of your day depends largely on whether you say: Good morning, God, or good god, morning.'

The last forty-two years have, in my experience, shown these words to be true. You need to get up praising God for the fact that your eyes are open afresh, praise Him for your breakfast, lunch, dinner, bedtime cocoa, and everything that happens in between. When you go through difficult moments, weeks, or years, ask Him to help you because He will. God's promise to Joshua as he prepared to lead the Israelites into the Promised Land remains valid for everyone who follows Him because the Bible is living, active, and never out-of-date: 'Be strong and courageous. Do not be afraid; do not be discouraged, for the LORD your God will be with you wherever you go' (Josh: 1:9).

What's more, we know, as Irish songsmith Brian Houston puts it, that all the time 'God Is Good.'[1]

NOTES

Introduction

1. MacCormac, Tonya: 'Cerebral Palsy: An Early Years Guide' (The Cedar Foundation information literature, 1999).

Chapter One

1. 'Disability,' "Definition of disability under the Equality Act 2010," https://www.gov.uk/definition-of-disability-under-equality-act-2010.

Afterword

1. Brian Houston, 'God Is Good', *Shelter* (Brian Houston Songs, 2012) CD.

ABOUT THE AUTHOR

Diagnosed with cerebral palsy at the age of two, Joe Boyd has enjoyed a successful career in Christian and secular journalism. From 1997 to 2015, he was the lead Religious Affairs Correspondent with the *Ballymena Times* newspaper. In 2015, he moved to www.thechurchpage.com, a Christian-run news website that publishes stories about churches and Christian organisations across the island of Ireland.

Joe has also authored two books: *A Celebration of God's Kitchen*, which was released in 2017, followed by his autobiography, *Trading Places: From Hopelessness to Happiness* (Timeless Publications, March 2019).

Joe and his wife, Rachael, have been married since 2014 and reside in Ballymena.